Bitches Die First

A Girl's Guide to Surviving the Apocalypse

Written by: AJ Clingerman

Fight Hub Publishing

1140 N. State Road 135

Suite CD

Greenwood, IN 46142

info@TheFightHub.com

For questions or more information about special discounts or bulk purchases, please contact Fight Hub Publishing at info@TheFightHub.com or 1140 N. State Road 135 Suite CD Greenwood, IN 46142

Cover Design by Canaan.Shaffner@gmail.com

ISBN-13: 978-1477648841

ISBN-10: 1477648844

Acknowledgements

First I want to thank my amazing husband, James. With out him, my world wouldn't be worth surviving.

Writing acknowledgements is very difficult. There have been so many people that have shaped me into who I am today. Some people because of their love and support and some because their doubt in me fuelled my fire.

I'm also terrified that I'll forget someone that is super important to me, but I want to give it a go…

Special thanks to
My Momma and my Grandma Helen – you two were the first strong, independent women in my life.

MH for starting my drive to want to be in charge of my own life.

Scott Manning for pushing me to be more than I thought I could be.

Suzanne Shafer, Krista Tharp, Cindy Dunston-Quirk and Jamie Johnson for kicking my butt into gear to get this book done.

My Peeps. Tina, Lish, Risser, Michelle, Jenn, and Bubs (deserter) for being the best girl friends a girl could ever ask for. People would be lucky to have one friend as amazing as any one of you, and I get six.

In addition, I'd like to thank Risser for helping me out with this book. I'm sure editing it was a nightmare, and I apologize for anything you told me to change that I didn't. ;-)

Fat Chicks and Skinny Bitches Die First

I realize the title alone is going to piss some people off and honestly – I'm okay with it. I'm not trying to write this book to make friends. I'm writing it to help women survive the Apocalypse (while providing a little entertainment while I'm at it). Let's be honest – if women don't survive, it will truly be the end of the world.

So save your letters on why you're fat or skinny and why you think you can still survive. I didn't say you wouldn't. I'm just saying Fat Chicks and Skinny Bitches Die First.

I Will Survive

I don't know about you, but I'm way too stubborn to lie down and die when the "Apocalypse" comes. I don't like being told what to do. I'm a take-charge kind of girl. I don't let brainless bloodsuckers rule me on a daily basis now so, there's no way I'm going to in the future.

The "Apocalypse" can come in many different forms; the zombie one is the most popular. I think it's because deep down we all like the idea of possibly getting to double tap our boss or jerk of a neighbor. What ever the reason is that we have to go into survival mode, I wanted to make sure that, as women, we are well prepared. I've got a great core group of girlfriends, lovingly referred to as the Peeps. They are all strong independent women, and I hope that they will be just as prepared to survive as I am, because life without them would suck. I hope the same for you and your girlfriends.

I've thought long and hard about what it's going to take to survive, and while that may make me sound crazy, you are reading this book, so who's crazy now?

I'm kidding. I think it's awesome that you are concerned about your own survival during the Apocalypse. Some people might think you are a little off your rocker for preparing for something that may never come, and while they are right that it may never come – I guarantee that by following the tips in this book, not only will you be prepared for anything, you will be a better, stronger person.

It may not be the end of the world, just the end of the world as we know it.

Is That What You Are Wearing?!?!

Girl! You cannot survive the Apocalypse in that! You look fabulous though! If you aren't willing to keep a change of clothing on you, I guess you'll make a hot zombie at least.

I understand. I dress up every day. I wear a suit or a dress and of course heels. If I have to run and jump and climb in that though…I'm not going to last the day. I have a hard enough time sitting at my desk in those clothes.

Let's talk about what you need to keep with you….

First of all – good, comfortable shoes. These may be the shoes that you wear for the rest of your life! You need to be able to walk all day, run when needed, climb, jump, and maybe kick some butt in them. No one is going to care how good your legs looked in those shoes when you are lying dead on the road.

Another thing I find almost as important is a hair tie. If you have long hair, this is a must. I can't stand watching the cop shows or superhero movies where the girl is running and fighting off bad guys with her hair down. Seriously?!?! It's going to get in your way. It'll be in your mouth and you could choke, or in your eyes so that you can't see, and worst yet – it can be used as something for someone to grab a hold of. When the Apocalypse comes, I figure I'll cut all my hair off, but until I get to a safe spot to do that, I'm going to have a hair tie on my wrist to pull it back.

Depending on where you are and what the season is when the Apocalypse hits, layers are important. Remember that all the clothing you own will either be on your body or something you are carrying. Be prepared. Some good gloves are a good plan. Even if it's not cold, you may want them to protect your hands. And I don't know about you, but I'm going with a good sports bra. Think about all that running…no one wants a black eye.

When you are thinking about exactly what your wardrobe will consist of, make sure that it's tight fitting clothing (to your body so you can move and not get caught up on things or people, not so that you can't get into them), that it's appropriate for the climate, and that you are prepared to wear it for weeks on end. Not pleasant, I know…but the end of the world never is.

Rule Number 1 – Cardio

I loved the movie Zombieland. It was very entertaining and yet really did teach us some very important lessons. Let's be honest – Cardio really is going to be one of the most important things you are going to need in order to survive. I hate to admit it, but I've always said how much I hate running and that "if I were ever being chased, I better know how to fight." While I still believe knowing some self-defense is important, I realized that I better be able to run. Whether I am trying to get away from zombies or marauders, I'm going to have to run.

If you are in a group and everyone is running, how bad are you going to feel if you are the weakest link and someone has to slow down to protect you? Are you willing to put not only your life in danger, but also the lives of those around you? Seriously girl – for yourself and those you love – let's start running.

Don't start off too fast. Your body will hate you and you'll hate running even more. You need to ease into a program gradually and you need to start today. You want to survive, right?

Start by doing some walking and jogging –

*Side Note – Being able to walk all day is also very important. Do you think you could do that now? Do you think you could walk from sun up to sun down? Could you do it with supplies on your back? In addition to the running training that we are about to go over – I recommend that you go out and spend at least an entire day per month hiking.

DISCLAIMER Talk to your doctor before starting any exercise program.

Back to running –

Start by doing some walking and jogging –

All you need to set aside is about 20-30 minutes 3x's a week for this.

They say the average American spends 34 hours a week watching TV! That's practically a full time job! Let's back off the television a little and get to training! I mean we need to get used to not watching TV anyway, right? I doubt there will be much during the Apocalypse!

Be sure to stretch before and after, even if you are mostly walking. If you are a Zombieland fan, you may remember that Rule Number 18 is Limber Up. It's important to stretch and get your body ready for the work you are about to do.

I recommend after doing a brisk 5-minute walk that you jog/walk in a 1:2 ratio. Start out jogging for 1 minute and walking for 2, alternating for a total of 20-30 minutes. Do that for the first week (3 workouts).

In the second week increase your jog time. Try out a 1.5:2 ratio. Jog for a minute and a half and then walk for two. You may want to only do 20 minutes of this when you are starting out. You can always increase the time as you build up.

In the third week try 1:1. Jog for 2 minutes and walk for 2 minutes. The important part is that each week you are increasing your jogging time. Build up to go longer and longer. As you increase the time you can jog, start decreasing the time that you walk in between until you are able to jog for the entire 30 minutes!

If you are anything like me you probably hate running, but THIS WILL SAVE YOUR LIFE!!!

Fight Like a Girl

Since we are talking about things that will save your life (I know, the whole book is about that), let's talk about learning to defend yourself.

It doesn't have to be the end of the world for you to protect your own life and learn self-defense.

When someone mentions self-defense there are a lot of things that come to mind. I'm sure there is some McDojo in your town that teaches some form of self-defense that in my opinion is more likely to get you killed. Most of that stuff is crap. If you aren't learning real world techniques that you can actually use and practice doing, they aren't going to do you a bit of good when you are attacked.

You may think I'm being vague here, so let me clear it up for you a bit. Learn some Brazilian Jiu Jitsu first. In my opinion (see my attempt at being politically correct here?), Brazilian Jiu Jitsu – also know as BJJ, is the best form of self-defense period, and especially for a woman. I can't stand when

11

people try to teach a woman to strike her attacker and actually expect it to help her survive. What's actually going to happen is you are going to piss him off even more. Maybe he was going to rape you or mug you, but now that you pissed him off, he might just kill you. How about instead we learn to defend ourselves, get back on our feet, and get the eff away!

Side Note: If you think I'm worked up about this it's because I am, and you should stop and think for a minute about how much I've toned this down. ;-)

Do I suggest that you also learn some striking? Absolutely!

I recommend some Muay Thai style Kickboxing. It's the most destructive form of striking. Also, as women, we are usually stronger in our legs. We would be able to develop more power in our kicks than we ever would be able to in our hands. And even if you are not able to effectively strike a man trying to attack you, you should be able to effectively strike a zombie. We are talking the end of the world here!!! If you are fighting off a zombie, breaking his knee with a good kick to the leg might give you just enough time to turn and run!

So there you have it. Learn some BJJ and Muay Thai. At the very least, take a Women's Self-Defense Seminar from a REPUTABLE BJJ school. This may save your life long before the Apocalypse.

Boom Boom Pow

Since we have been talking so much about the physical aspect, I figure now is a good time to discuss weapons.

I'll be really honest with you…I've always been afraid of guns. They freaked me out as a kid and when I was about 20, my boyfriend (now husband) was sitting at a stop light and got shot in the head with a 9mm by a complete stranger. They had never even met in traffic before the light. It was just some drunk idiot that was trying to be a tough guy and start stuff. I'm very thankful that my husband lived through the ordeal. If you met him today, you wouldn't even know that anything had ever happened. Even 12 years after that when I saw a 9mm up close for the first time, I cried. It's hard to explain, and maybe you understand already, but they just freaked me out.

I knew that the only way I was going to be able to be comfortable with them was to learn to use them properly. So over the last year, every chance I've gotten, I've shot every gun I could (yeah, it took me

12 years to get to that point). Do they still freak me out? Yes. They should. They are deadly weapons, but if I ever have to use one, I'm going to need to know how.

Think about the movies...

There's some threat, they find a stockpile of guns, and they just start throwing them out to everyone. Can you imagine if the chick in the movie caught the gun and said "I'm afraid of guns" or "I don't know what to do with this thing"? In an emergency situation there is no time for that. You better know what you are doing and you better be less afraid of shooting the gun than you are of whatever you are shooting at.

You need to learn how to shoot it, load it, and clean it. There are plenty of places that offer classes in shooting different kinds of guns. Do I recommend that you have a gun of your own? Well, since I am exercising my First Amendment right (Freedom of Speech), I will tell you that I myself exercise my Second Amendment right (Right to Bear Arms). Whether you do or not is your choice.

If you have a gun or not, you are going to want to have some additional weapons, especially since bullets run out. By the way – I suggest you use bullets only when it's your only choice – conservation is key.

I highly recommend a crowbar. It will make for a good defense mechanism as well as help you to move stuff and get in safe places, which are both imperative to your survival.

I also believe that you are going to need some blades. A machete makes for a great weapon and can help you clear some brush to make a fire. Knives can help you not only defend yourself, but cut the meat that you have caught to eat.

Remember that everything you have, you have to be able to carry. Multipurpose tools and weapons are always the best way to go!

A Girl's Gotta Eat

Wouldn't it suck if you survived whatever disaster it was that brought on the Apocalypse only to starve to death!?!?!

This is part of why I think that skinny bitches die first. They aren't going to have any stored fat for reserves. The skinny ones also probably don't have a lot of energy and strength to keep going.

But you, you are going to survive. There is so much you are going to need to know to be able to feed yourself.

Let's start with the easy stuff –

Know what fruits and vegetables grow in the region you are in. Is there an orchard near by? What about a large garden or field with vegetables? Obviously this will only help if it's near harvest time. That's what makes it the easy stuff.

There are lots of plants that you can eat. Did you know that you can eat dandelions? How about roses? When I was a kid I remember that we used to have this big poster of edible plants and I used to go around and try to find them so that I could try them. None of them were things I wanted to eat on a regular basis, but that's because we live in a cush society. If it were the end of days, dandelions would look mighty tasty.

Avoid plants near the road because they will be laden with contamination from exhaust emissions. I know you'll want to eat any food that you come across that you recognize, but if it's starting to spoil or show signs of mildew and fungus, you need to avoid it. Some plants can develop extremely dangerous fungal toxins. You should also avoid any plants that have an almond scent to them…that's a characteristic of cyanide compounds.

Do not eat wild mushrooms! Unless you can positively identify the edible ones versus the ones that cause central nervous system issues. Do you know that the symptoms can take days to show up? You could have been eating them every day, thinking they are perfectly fine. Seriously, just avoid them.

Just to be safe – avoid any unknown or wild plants that have spines, fine hairs, thorns, bitter taste, pods with seeds, bulbs or beans, soapy taste, milky sap, three leaved growth pattern….

Honestly, I suggest you do some research online or pick up a little guidebook on plants that you can eat.

Now it gets harder…

You are going to need protein. You have to have it to keep your energy up and you need it to survive. Even a vegetarian is getting protein in his or her diet currently through beans, legumes, powders, etc. But those things aren't going to be as easy to come by. You are going to need to learn to hunt, trap, and fish.

I fished a lot with my dad when I was a kid. I'm sure I mostly played in the water and scared the fish

19

away. I never witnessed the fish dying and eating them didn't bother me too much…but a deer…or a rabbit…that stuff made me so sad. Who could kill and eat Bambi and Thumper? If it meant survival? I could. I mentioned before that I go shooting whenever I can. I do target practice so that if I ever need to shoot an animal, I have a better chance at actually hitting it.

Also, research some various ways of trapping animals. Just remember that most times you will still have to kill the animal. Will you shoot it (remember bullets are in limited supply)? Or will you use your machete on it? It's not going to be pretty or fun, but hey, it's the end of the world.

Grab a Partner

I know that if I have to kill an animal to survive, I will, but my hope is actually that my husband will do it.

I bring this up because if you are going to survive the end of the world you are going to need an able and ready partner for it. I don't care if you prefer a man or a woman. Just make sure your partner is going to aid you and not hinder your survival. Also, make sure that it's someone that you actually want to spend the end of days with.

I'm lucky enough to (even after 13 years) be in one of those sappy relationships where we can be together all the time and I still miss him when I have to leave the room to go pee. There's not going to be a lot of alone time during the Apocalypse (in fact there should be none), so are you ready to spend every minute of every day with your partner?

I'm also lucky that my husband is as prepared or more (especially on the self-defense aspect) as I am.

You can't be this crazy about being prepared and be with someone who isn't just as crazy.

Even though this book is geared to helping women survive the Apocalypse, your man should be taking the advice too. He should be able to run. He needs to know self-defense. He better be able to use a weapon and know how to hunt and gather. He needs to know the proper clothes to wear. I'm guessing he doesn't wear heels and may not need a hair tie, but still, this is all important stuff for him too.

All I'm saying is: make sure that your partner is as prepared as you are!

Tie the Knot

Since we just discussed the perfect partner I thought it led nicely into tying the knot. I'm actually not talking about marriage.

I want to make sure that you can actually tie some knots.

Again, let's start easy.

Braiding. Do you know how to braid? If you have long hair, this will come in handy with keeping it back until you are ready to chop it off. Also, braiding will make any rope stronger.

If you don't already know how to braid, it's pretty easy. Section hair (or rope) into three pieces, take right side over the middle, then the left side over the new middle. Keep going all the way down. A French braid is basically the same, but you start with a small section of hair and divide it into three, as you go pick up a little more hair each time. It's really all about figuring out how to hold it with your fingers. The concept isn't difficult; it just takes some practice. If you want to see it being done, check out my Youtube page – www.YouTube.com/TheApocalypseChick.

The next thing I suggest you know how to do is make a paracord bracelet. You can order 100 feet of paracord online for like $15. I got some in a ton of different colors – of course black, army green, gray…but I also got blue, pink, purple, neon green, orange…all kinds of fun colors. Once you get the hang of it you can have a bracelet done in less than 15 minutes. I made one for all my friends and family for Christmas. It reminded me a lot of when I was a kid and I used to make friendship bracelets. It was a lot of fun and you can use them not only as bracelets, but as key chains, or straps, whatever. And in a survival situation, you can unwind them and use them for trapping, hanging clothes to dry, tying up shelter and anything else you can imagine. It's 10 feet of rope that holds 550lbs around your wrist! What more can you ask for?!?!

Maybe longer rope! I kept thinking…what if I needed more than the 10 feet around my wrist…. So I made my husband a belt! It's 100 feet of paracord! And it turned out great! I did not use the same knot that I used in making the bracelets. See the problem with the bracelets is that it will take some time to untie it to use, but with the belt, I basically crocheted it! With a good tug I could get it all undone and ready for use in a matter of a couple minutes! I feel really good about that!

For more information on this whole tying the knot thing, I suggest that you check out my YouTube Channel –
www.YouTube.com/TheApocalypseChick

Get Your Beauty Rest

Girl you look like death!

Worst thing to hear when you are surrounded by zombies.

Don't make the mistake of thinking that you can go days on end without sleep. That may have worked in college, but the English final was much easier than fighting off zombies and marauders is going to be!

Always have someone stay up and keep watch. If you have a large group, I suggest that you take shifts and have a couple people keeping watch at a time. You'll be safer and everyone will get a chance to get some rest.

If you are by yourself or just with your partner – still take shifts, but prop yourself up against a wall or tree. Try to be somewhere where you can't be snuck up on. Sleep with your weapons and

ALWAYS sleep with your shoes on. You have to be ready to run or fight if need be.

Seriously, make sure that you are getting some sleep. You are going to need it.

Don't Bleed to Death

It's very important that you learn some basic first aid. I'm sure you have some medical supplies in your bug out bag. You need to know how to make a tourniquet and how to cauterize a wound. There's no room for not being able to stomach blood. You are going to have to deal with it.

Guys that are reading this guide – you may want to skip this next section. It doesn't concern you...

Girls – in addition to wounds you are going to have to deal with other things bleeding. Now, there is a good chance that with all the stress of the end of the world, your body will actually not go through its cycle, meaning that you will not have periods. This is called amenorrhea and at this point, you are hoping for it. But on the off chance that you don't get AMENorrhea, you are going to want to have some tampons in your bug out bag. You are only going to be able to take so many, and they are only going to last you so long, but having them is going to be so much better than not.

In the "olden days" women used cloth or rags (it's where the term being on the rag came from), stuffed up in there. When one got filled they put in a new one and washed that one out. Sounds like fun, right? I guess you've got to do what you've got to do, huh?

There are actually modern versions of this – reusable pads. Not my cup of tea, for sure. Some women do actually currently use these, obviously they are better for the environment, so I won't knock them, but there are far easier, less gross things to recycle. I guess maybe I should get some for my bug out bag though…just in case.

There is also some sort of cup that you can use. You put it up there and it catches the blood. When it's full, you simply (I'm guessing not really simply), get it out, empty it (I'm hoping wash it), and put it back in.

You thought being on your period was a bitch now….

Going back to the whole tampon thing, they are good for other things – like wounds, stopping nosebleeds, fire kindling, and earplugs. While my first thought was that I wouldn't waste a tampon on any of these things, my second thought was mentioning these awesome uses might just be a good way to get my husband to carry some in his bug out bag for me. Super score!

Cabin Fever

It's the end of the world as we know it, and I feel fine.

Sometimes part of surviving is having some normalcy in your life. You are going to need a way to keep not only yourself, but also those in your party entertained.

A pack of cards in your bug out bag will be a good start. Other great things to do will be to play charades, tell stories and jokes, and sing songs. It may seem silly now, and maybe it's not something that you would do in your everyday life, but you have to find ways to keep yourselves entertained.

Cabin Fever is a real thing (haven't you seen *The Shining*?) and you don't want to have done all of this only to go crazy from boredom.

One of my life mottos is 'So long as you are willing to act like a fool, you'll always have a good time.' I think this still rings true, all the way to the end of time.

Rules to Live By

I don't know about you, but when I first started driving, my mom always told me to make sure that I never had less than half of a tank of gas. "Think of the half way point as empty," she would say. That way if I ever got stuck anywhere, I would always have plenty of gas to keep the heat on. She also always had me keep a blanket in the car – just in case.

Let's be honest – who doesn't suck at keeping their gas above the half way mark?!?! I drive a lot, and that would mean stopping for gas nearly every day. If I look at it like trying not to get stranded, I let it go all the way down until the thing dings, but if I were to look at it like – In the middle of the night tonight, something may happen and I may have to drive as far as I can with out stopping. Or tomorrow, I may have to survive the Apocalypse. – Well…then maybe I'm more likely to go ahead and stop to fill 'er up.

Along with your gas tank being full, your cell phone should have a good charge. Again – I'm guilty of not plugging it in at night and browsing the Internet and texting all day. But what if it's life or death and you don't have your phone charged? Think about 9/11 for a minute…. How many people were able to call their loved ones (before the towers got all jammed) and tell them that they loved them? Wouldn't you want to make sure that if given that option, you could take it? What if there is some catastrophe and you need to call your loved ones and make sure that they are able to meet you at your pre-arranged rendezvous point? Do you have enough charge to do so? Do they?

Another rule to live by is be aware of your surroundings. When you are walking to your car alone, when you are going out to check the mail when you get home at night, when you are walking into the store or loading groceries into you car…. At all times, be aware of your surroundings.

I think about that statement 'if it were a snake it would have bitten me' – what if it were 'if it were a zombie it would have bitten me' – changes everything. While you may think of the whole zombie thing as a bit of a joke, this is still über important to your survival. A woman who pays attention to her surroundings is far less likely to get attacked, and I'm not talking about the walking dead here.

Kick the addictions now. I personally am a caffeine addict; I hate to admit it, but I know it's true. I need to kick that now! Have you ever quit drinking caffeine? Even for those of you that just drink some pop and not the hard-core energy drinks like I like, have you ever given it up? You have a terrible headache for the first 2-3 days! Think about it for a minute…. Those first 2-3 days are going to be some of the roughest as it is. Those are the days that you are trying to get away from the scenario. If you can survive those first 72 hours, you have a pretty good chance of long-term survival. Now what if you have to go through those first few days with a massive, caffeine withdrawal headache…? It's going to be rough.

But there are worse things…. Do you currently drink alcohol every day? Have you ever seen anyone go through DTs? It's not pretty. It's terrible, in fact. People die just from going through it. You go through it in a survival situation and you can just take out that word survival. And if you have loved ones with you, you know they are going to try to keep you safe while you go through it…now you've just decreased their chances as well.

It's a horrible situation and I'm just telling you now – while you have all the luxuries in the world – kick the addictions.

When the $#!^ Hits the Fan

There are a lot of things that you and your family are going to need to plan out for when it all goes down. I'm just going to give you a brief overview of what I want to make sure you don't miss.

Have a fully developed plan. If you are separated at work or whatever, know how and where you are going to meet up. If you have kids in school or at sitters, know who is getting them and how. Do you have your bug out bag with you? Is it in your car or at your house? It's all got to be planned. If you live in the city and have to take a train to work, can you keep a second bug out bag at work? Can you hide one where you are meeting up (this should not be your only one in case you can't make it there)? I repeat – it must all be planned.

Stay calm. As women we are very emotional creatures. There is no time for tears right now. Suck it up girl. You have to be strong. You can't get hysterical. You have planned for this. Stick to the plan and don't lose it.

Bug Out

I keep mentioning various things that you should have in your bug out bag, so let's go through all of it!

It's important that you make yourself (and your loved ones if necessary), bug out bags that can stay just that. Designate durable backpacks that you won't need to empty out to use for anything else.

Here's what I've mentioned so far –

_____ **A copy of this guide book**, just in case you forget anything.

_____ **Change of clothing** – form fitting, comfortable layers, maybe some gloves and perhaps a good sports bra. Include an extra pair of socks.

_____ **Good shoes** – shoes that you can run, jump, and climb in. They don't need to be cute; they need to be functional.

_____ **Hair ties** – No one can really fight zombies or marauders with her hair in her face.

_____ **Weapons** – crowbar, blades – (e.g.: machete), perhaps a gun.

_____ **Seeds**

_____ **Paracord**

_____ **Plant guide**

_____ **First Aid Supplies** (full list in separate section)

_____ Tampons

Here is what I also have in my bug out bag –

_____ **Water filter** – I love the bottles with the built-in filters. I take these with me on airplanes so that I can fill up with water after I go through security. They work really well. I will suggest that you also have a couple of bottles of water just in case.

_____ **Iodine tablets** – We're still talking about clean water here. You can't survive with out it.

_____ **Food** – I have some packages of tuna, trailmix, energy bars, and beef jerky. You should also look into some MREs or complete meals.

_____ **Bandanas**

_____ **Solar blankets** – you can get like 12 of these for $10 on Amazon.

_____ **Poncho** to stay dry.

_____ **Matches, Emergency Fire starter**

_____ **Small pan/large cup** to boil water for filtering and heating food.

_____ **Multi-tool**

_____ **Flashlights and extra batteries**

_____ **Mirror** (could be used for signaling)

_____ **Hand crank radio and flashlight**

_____ **Anti-Diarrhea medication** – 1) you don't have time for that $#!^ and 2) it could lead to dehydration very quickly, especially when water is scarce.

_____ **Compass**

_____ **Fishing lures and line**

_____ **Duct tape** – good for nearly everything.

_____ **Cash** – depending on the situation, it could come in handy, and even if society has fallen and it has no real value anymore, many people will have trouble giving up that notion. You could buy yourselves some survival musts.

_____ **Fingernail clippers**

_____ **Sewing kit** – needle and thread.

_____ **Wire saw**

_____ **Toothbrush and Toothpaste**

_____ **Soap**

_____ **Hand Sanitizer**

_____ **Toilet Paper**

_____ **Ear Plugs**

_____ **Electrolyte Powder**

_____ **Pens**

_____ **Whistle**

_____ **Bag of Dryer Lint** (great for starting a fire)

_____ **Bug Repellant**

_____ **Gas Mask**

_____ **Tiny Tweezers** (you may need to remove a tick)

_____ **Pepper Spray** (you never know)

First Aid Kit

Let's not consider this an exhaustive list. This is just a good base...something to start with. Make sure you have these items at a minimum. You can always add more, especially if you have specific circumstances e.g.: you need an inhaler or an epipen.

_____ Roll of Flexwrap

_____ Roll of Medical Tape

_____ Ace Bandage

_____ Bandaids

_____ Antiseptic

_____ Anti-Diarrhea Medicine

_____ Iodine pills

_____ Sterile Gauze

_____ Bottle of Newskin

Let Me Entertain You

As discussed in the section Cabin Fever – you are going to want to play some game to keep yourself and your crew entertained. Use the next few pages to play Tic Tac Toe (play small – use your space), or perhaps that dot game – you know the one – you make like 12 dots (or whatever number you chose) in a square and you draw a line from one dot to another. When you make a square you write your initials in it and draw another line!

Let Me Entertain You

Let Me Entertain You

Notes

Take the next few pages to think about what your plan will be. Talk about it with your friends and family. When there is an emergency – be it Apocalypse, zombie attack, or even flood, hurricane, earthquake, tsunami, whatever – what is your plan? Could you survive for a few days while waiting for help?

Sure this guide is all a little tongue in cheek, but it's serious too. I want you to survive!

Notes

Notes

About the Author

AJ Clingerman, along with her husband James own and operate the Indiana Brazilian Jiu Jitsu Academy, the Extreme Grappling Open and www.TheFightHub.com. In addition to many other endeavors, AJ enjoys dancing, acting, and just about anything outdoorsy and active. She has two pretty cool brothers (Alex and Joey), three lovely sisters (Brit, Heather and Candice) and one super awesome nephew (Devo). AJ has written many other books, including These Three Miracles, The Unfrozen and The Story of Us…This is just the first one she has actually finished.

Please be sure to check out her YouTube page at www.YouTube.com/TheApocalypseChick. Also check out www.FightHubHQ.com and please feel free to come in and train with her!

Made in the USA
Lexington, KY
15 July 2012